DEATH & RESURRECTION

Comprising

DEATH

Leonard Cheshire VC

1978

THE RESURRECTION

Bede Jarrett OP

1919

CATHOLIC TRUTH SOCIETY

PUBLISHERS TO THE HOLY SEE

To accompany a man on his final life's steps…is to receive as much as it is to give. It is to become more of a man oneself.

Leonard Cheshire (1917-1992) was a war hero who after the war spent his life caring for the sick and dying. Bede Jarrett (1881-1934) was a well-known historian and spiritual writer.

CTS ONEFIFTIES
Originally published as *Death*, 1978; and *The Resurrection*, 1919.
Published by The Incorporated Catholic Truth Society,
40-46 Harleyford Road, London SE11 5AY
www.ctsbooks.org
Copyright © 2017 The Incorporated Catholic Truth Society.

ISBN 978 1 78469 530 9

DEATH

Leonard Cheshire VC

INTRODUCTION

There are many who have dedicated their lives to the care of the dying and who are qualified to write with authority. With my own limited involvement with those who are dying, I cannot claim to come into this category. Yet, whoever has sat by a deathbed and participated, even if only in total silence, in another person's journey into the unknown has something to offer to the totality of our knowledge of what dying involves, for no two deaths can be entirely the same any more than can two individual human lives. It is solely because I believe this to be true that I have responded to the suggestion that I place on record something of my own experience with those who are about to leave this life, as well as the conclusions that I have drawn from it.

I feel tempted to say that of all the acts that we perform during our lifetime, the act of dying is perhaps the most personal of all. Above all it is personal in the sense that the manner in which we die brings to consummation and gives a final, irrevocable direction to our life for all eternity. It is also personal in the sense that it contains a hidden element known only to God and to the person concerned. There takes place in the uttermost depth of our being a dialogue into which no one else on earth, even our closest partner, the sharer of all our other secrets, can enter. This is not to say that others cannot strengthen and support us, and even share or guide some of our conscious thoughts: indeed they can and indeed they should. But death, it seems to me, is essentially a personal encounter which we, so far as this world is concerned, have to conduct on our own. It is, we know, a personal encounter with God, and God, we also know, is a God of love. We may therefore think that it will prove a loving and merciful encounter, the end of our trial and tribulations and the beginning of eternal happiness. So, in the ultimate sense, it undoubtedly will be. But everything that I have both read and experienced forces me to assert that God is totally beyond our comprehension. Whenever he intervenes in human history, at whatever level and in whatever way, he invariably seems to leave man bemused and uncomprehending.

From the opening chapter of Holy Scripture to its very last, despite all that God has revealed to us about himself and our relationship with him throughout the whole of human history, and despite the immense volume of prayer, thought and study that the believing world has given to this ever unfolding revelation, we still fail to recognise God for what he really is, even the very best of us. How poignant, and also how revealing, is the cry of Jesus faced at the end of his life's work, as he was, by the incredulity of his apostles: 'What, Philip, here have I been all this time with you and still you do not recognise me.' How equally poignant that other cry seven centuries earlier when Judah after her years of exile in Babylon had still not learnt her lesson: 'For my thoughts are not your thoughts, nor are your ways my ways, says the Lord. As high as the heavens are above the earth, so high are my ways above your ways and my thoughts above your thoughts.' Only when our own time for that encounter with our Creator has arrived will the real significance of those twin cries be brought home to us. For each of us that encounter at the hour of our death will be a supremely personal moment, different and individual for every single human being. But it will be a moment, I believe, not when the book is just closed and everything so far as our part is concerned over and done with, but a moment when something will be asked of us, when there will be a decision that we must take and some action to which we must make a commitment. In any event there will simultaneously take place another encounter of a different order, that between the person that God willed us to be and which, had we allowed the divine life of Grace to reach its full plenitude within us, we could have been, and the person that we actually are. That in itself must inevitably call for some urgent steps to be taken. Thus the first thing that needs to be said about death is that it is not merely the act of a spoiler striking from without–though that indeed it is–it is also and most fundamentally of all an interior act of our own, a response on our side to the choice that death, the spoiler, sets before us. If not actually the most personal, certainly it is the most significant of all the acts that we are ever called upon to make.

A PERSONAL EXPERIENCE

Although I served for some five years with the wartime Bomber Command where death in one form or another was virtually a daily visitor, my own involvement with a dying person did not come about until a few months after my thirtieth birthday. It began with an unexpected telephone call from the Matron of the local hospital, at Petersfield in Hampshire, to tell me that an old man, Arthur Dykes, whom I knew slightly, was dying of cancer. There was nothing more to be done for him from a medical or nursing point of view, merely to care for him, feed him and wash him, and since the hospital had a longish waiting list they could no longer afford to keep his bed. He had no known relatives and no contact address other than mine, and yet somebody had to take responsibility for him. Although ten years older than call-up age, he had enlisted in the R.A.F. as a Nursing Orderly, and in view of this I had little hesitation in agreeing to find an alternative place, thinking that all that would be required would be a nicely worded letter to one or other of the Ex-Service Organisations.

When I reported to the hospital, the Matron, in giving me the information and details that she felt I would need, told me very emphatically that under no circumstances was I to give him any indication of the fact that he had not long to live. To be perfectly honest, I was somewhat relieved at this, for the mere thought that it might fall to me to break this news to him filled me with a sudden dread. As R.A.F. aircrew we had had no inhibitions in talking about death, either the possibility of our own or someone else's, or of what it must feel like when one finally realised that there was no hope of baling out of an aircraft about to crash. In every squadron in which I served there were one or two aircrew who spoke of a premonition that they would not survive. They tended to be the exception, for the majority of us were buoyed up by the belief, 'It can never happen to me'. But the fact remained that quite a number of those who spoke of having a premonition did end up by not coming back. In some cases it may really have been a genuine premonition: I do not know. In most cases, however, I think that their state of mind proved their undoing. That is to say when they were hit by a shell or when something seemed to have gone seriously wrong, their immediate reaction was: 'Yes, I knew it. This is it. Bale out.' The average man, on the other hand, would react very differently. His greatest hope was not to crash or to bale out over enemy territory, and therefore he would hold on in the hope that things were not quite as bad as they seemed. The instinct for survival is very strong and even if the situation is in fact desperate, it is extraordinary what a human being will do to extricate himself, as was proved time and time again throughout the war.

However, to return to my main theme, death in this sense, even if applied as a possible future happening to oneself, was a subject that we discussed as a purely hypothetical and abstract event. Looking into the eyes of the man who really was dying and talking to him about his own death in the immediate concrete present was a different thing altogether. Yes, I was relieved that the Matron had spoken as she had. She had done so with an air of authority, a member of the nursing profession speaking as a professional to me as a layman, and so I felt absolved from a responsibility which otherwise I might have gone through agonies of mind not knowing how to discharge. But during my conversation with Arthur, he told me that the doctors had completed their course of treatment, and advised him to rest so as to build up his strength and that already he was beginning to feel better. He realised that he would have to move from hospital and to my great dismay asked if I would let him have a little piece of land, big enough to hold a caravan and reasonably accessible to a road. By the time I returned for my second visit to report the progress I had made—or rather not made—in finding alternative hospital or nursing home accommodation, I had made up my mind that whatever else I did I could not allow him to continue to plan his future when in fact there was no future for which to plan. The seven mile drive from the large and rather lonely house where I was living was one of the most uncomfortable I can ever remember making. I deliberately avoided meeting the Matron, went straight to Athur's room, offered him a cigarette and lit one myself. I knew I would be lost if I allowed Arthur to lead me off into plans and proposals for the future, or indeed divert me in any way whatsoever, and yet I had to have just a few moments to settle and steel myself, and to try and establish some kind of rapport with him. In my nervousness I might well have just blurted the truth out, anything to get the load off my mind, but mercifully Arthur had a certain depth and composure to him that served to help me keep my head. So far as I can remember, I made some gesture to indicate that there was something special that I wanted to tell him and said: 'Arthur, I have had a word with the doctor and I feel I've got to tell you that he doesn't think you are going to get better.' There seemed nothing that I could possibly add, and so I just waited hoping with all my heart that Arthur would neither break down nor ask me to be more specific. He just sat looking at me for a moment or two and then seemed to settle back into the pillows and relax as if a huge burden had been taken off his shoulders. 'Thank you, Len, for telling me,' he said.

Telling the Truth

That little movement back into the pillows and those few simple words told me almost as much as any book or paper that I have since read about this aspect of dying.

First and foremost it showed me that Arthur had in fact suspected that all was not quite as well as the doctors had been telling him. It is common human experience that not to know where one stands in a matter where a great deal is at stake is one of the worst human situations. To begin with there is nothing solid upon which one can build even the flimsiest of shelters. One can plan neither for life nor for death. One moment finds us convinced that all will be well and that there is a more or less rosy future ahead. The next finds us thrown back into a maelstrom of doubt and inner questioning. One looks at the doctor searching for some clue as to what really is the truth. To the tip of one's tongue comes the question: 'Doctor, will you tell me the truth. It won't upset me: I just want to be sure.' Then one's mind is assailed with doubts. 'Will my question embarrass him? Is there some medical code by which he is bound? Is he perhaps unsure whether I actually mean what I am asking?' Whether the commonly held theory about drowning is true in the physical sense, that is to say that when the struggle is over and one's lungs fill with water there is no pain, I do not know. I do know, however, that from the mental point of view it is true. During the struggle to keep oneself alive when everything is dark, hopeless, squeezing the last ounce of one's strength, one's mind is in anguish and torment. But when the struggle is over, the evidence is that one's mind is suddenly at peace. A wartime fighter pilot who later rose to become Chief of the Air Staff described one day his experience of his aircraft being set on fire. Since it was a single-engined aircraft with the fire in the engine itself, and since he was too low to bale out, his only way of keeping alive was to veer the nose first to one side and then to the other so as to keep the flames from bursting into the cockpit. At one and the same time he had to watch his instruments to make certain that he was not stalling and try to see what lay ahead of him on the ground in the hope of avoiding a fatal crash. His mind, he said, was in an agony of torment, not only because it was his own life at stake but because he knew he had a duty to land intact so as to live to fight another day, and he could not tell whether he was handling the aircraft as he should. Then, despite his efforts, the flames defeated him and there was nothing to do but sit back and await whatever should happen. In that instant he suddenly found himself completely composed and at rest, his struggle finished and his destiny in other hands than his. By one of those miracles of fate that occasionally befall us, his Spitfire hit the ground without disintegrating, enabling him to escape and in due course to return to his squadron. One cannot, of course, generalise from the particular, nor can one equate the situation of a man in the full flood of life suddenly confronted by the prospect of sudden death with that of a man whose life is irreversibly ebbing away. But from what I have seen and experienced I believe that as a general principle it is true that the majority of us would rather know where we stand however harsh the truth may be than be left in doubt.

How to tell?

In the second place it was very clear to me that although there could be no possible question about the correctness–I feel like adding the morality–of telling Arthur where he stood, the question of how to tell him was another matter altogether. Inevitably I now talk with the benefit of hindsight, having had to break the same news to others, each of whose personal circumstances were so very different. Nevertheless, everything that I was to discover from my involvement with the others was, I think, implicit in my conversation with Arthur. Once I had overcome my feeling of panic at the realisation that it was something that I was going to have to do on my own with no one on earth to whom I could go for advice, I realised that I would have to manoeuvre myself into a position where it was he, not I, who led the conversation. Others, I am sure, will bear the same testimony, namely that one is treading on very personal, indeed very holy, ground. The actual telling must be done at a moment and in a manner that fits the other person's need. In some cases it may require a very gentle and slow approach, a hint here, a little pointer there, perhaps even an affirmation more by what is not said than by any positive disclosure. How, I have to ask myself, can anybody give even a guide line to another? The matter is so sensitive and so personal a one, that it can really only be left to the individual judgement, or rather intuition, of the person concerned. The surest course, perhaps, is to win the dying person's trust, to be ready to give him time and to be content to listen, leaving the subject he wants to talk about to him rather than impose one's own choice. True, there will be the man who consciously seeks to avoid the issue altogether, and here, depending upon the circumstances, it may be necessary to lead him, gently, if possible, but at all events lead him, to the point where he stands face to face with reality. If even then he turns his back on it there is nothing more one can do, but not to try at all would be to fail in a duty that each of us owes towards those of our own family circle and to those whom circumstances have placed in some special relationship to us.

I am fully aware that the man who holds no religious belief and sees death not as a gateway but as pure annihilation will answer that the less warning one has of this dread calamity the better. He may even enquire what right have we to impose our own private view of what lies beyond death upon a man who would prefer to be left undisturbed in his own belief that he possesses no such thing as an immortal soul. But we too can turn the same question back on him. What right has he got to impose what he acknowledges is only a belief, and refuse another person the opportunity to reassess his thinking now that for the first and only time in his life death is staring him in the face? Is the possible distress of mind that he may suffer to be measured against what he stands to lose if it turns out that he had in fact an immortal soul which now stands at the cross roads of life itself? However, these considerations apart, I can only speak from the experience of my own involvement with those who are dying, limited though I know it to be. By no means all of these have been professing Christians or indeed men of any faith or belief at all. Some have persisted in maintaining that they refuse to believe in any hereafter right up until the end–though not, I have a feeling, quite up to the end. It may, I have to acknowledge, be a purely subjective and ill-founded conclusion, or wishful thinking some might say, but somewhere during the last moments of semi-consciousness a subtle change seemed to come about. But what at least is true is that all wanted to know, and each in his own way seemed to want to talk about his point of view as if to put it to the test. There are others too whose family would confide in me that they had managed to keep the matter secret and that their husband or wife, or mother or whoever it might be had no idea of the true state of their health. I think they were all wrong. I am almost certain that in every instance the person did know, though in such a situation, as a mere outsider, it would have been unthinkable to intervene, at any rate without the family's permission. I heard of one such instance where the dying husband broke down in front of a visiting social worker and said: 'I know that I am dying, but I can't discuss it with my wife who has shared everything all our married lives. She just insists on pretending that all is well.'

The dignity of the dying

Although at the time I was not aware of it, and even had I been I doubt that it would have meant much to me, Arthur Dykes was a Catholic who had abandoned his faith. From the moment that he looked me in the eyes and thanked me for having told him where he stood, I felt that a personal bond had been forged between us. Little did I guess what the future would hold, both for Arthur and myself, in consequence of this conversation, but I realised that the man in front of me had suddenly become a different person from the one I had visited a week or so before. In a subtle kind of way he had acquired a new dignity and a new authority. Whereas previously our conversation had roamed first here, then there, without any discernible theme or purpose, now he had the air of a man who knew what he was about. My expectation of finding a hospital or nursing home bed for him proved unrealisable, and so it came about that the last three months of his life were spent in my own house, and that we were alone together at the moment of his death.

The first indication that death was approaching came in the early afternoon of a warm and sunny August day. Arthur must have been born with a very strong physical constitution and remarkable determination, if not sheer obstinacy. Despite his by now almost unbelievably wasted and skinny body, he still insisted on using a commode instead of a bedpan, even though he required help and support to get there and back. On this occasion we were half way back to the bed when he suddenly stiffened and looked as if he was going to collapse. Rather misguidedly, as I have since thought, I told him not to worry, just to let himself go and relax, and without waiting for a reply made to pick him up. Instead of letting me do so, however, he tried to resist, with the result that he suffered what I supposed to have been an internal haemorrhage and cried out a rather agonised 'Lumme'. It was obvious as soon as I had got him back into bed that something serious had happened and that death could not be very far away. I telephoned first the hospital to ask if there was anything special that I ought to do and then the Catholic priest, for Arthur had by now regained his faith and on more than one occasion had asked me what sensible reason could I adduce for not becoming a Catholic myself!

A final decision?

Throughout the six or seven hours that I sat with him in his room punctuated only by Father Clarke's visit to administer the Last Sacraments, the two of us hardly exchanged a single sentence. Arthur was conscious and half sitting up against the pillows which I had arranged as comfortably as possible, but he gave the impression of hardly knowing that I was there at all. For my part I felt completely at a loss to know what to say or do. It had been self-evident for some time that sooner or later this moment would come, and I suppose that I had tried to picture what it would be like and what I ought to say, rather piously hoping that I would find something edifying or uplifting. But now that the actual moment was upon me, I realised my total inadequacy. The best I could manage was something like, 'Is there anything I can get you?' or 'Would you like a cigarette?' Arthur would turn his head to look at me, but so far as I can remember he never answered. What I was saying clearly had no relevance to his particular situation. Indeed I began to suspect that the occasional remarks I was making were a distraction to him, and an intrusion upon something very personal that was taking place inside him. Although only semi-conscious and clearly becoming steadily weaker, his expression was thoughtful and intelligent, with a certain puzzled look in his eyes which I could not quite identify. For all the world he was a man who was holding a conversation on a matter of unusual importance, but it was not to me that he was talking, nor was I in any way connected with the inner, mysterious dialogue that totally absorbed his thoughts. It slowly dawned on me that what he in fact was doing was facing up to a decision. Yet there was some element in the making of it that evidently surprised him, for which he gave the impression of not being prepared. I had watched him steadily regain his faith over the past three months or so and had been profoundly impressed both by his serenity and by the simple yet authoritative way in which he could answer profound questions relating to religious belief. A humble man, he had faced his impending death in a way that was totally convincing: never once did I hear him say anything that jarred or that smacked of the over-pious. Whatever may have lain in his past, he was now a man of Faith in the best and truest sense. Yet here he was confronted with something that mystified him, something, I had a feeling, that was calling for a difficult decision. The only words he spoke, or at least the only ones I can remember, if anything made the situation more obscure to me rather than the reverse. With an air partly of wonderment and partly of profound thoughtfulness, he turned his face towards me and said: 'Yes, I suppose that I shall have to go.' I can only record what I saw and heard and the effect that this had on me at the time. In the light of what I have subsequently experienced and from what others have themselves recorded or written, I can perhaps offer a possible interpretation of what Arthur was in fact turning over in his mind, but necessarily this must remain a purely personal and subjective view.

DEATH: ITS INNER NATURE

Our attitude to death must of course depend upon the view we hold about the nature and the ultimate destiny of man. I myself can only speak as I see and believe it to be, that is to say as a Christian, making my three or four assertions without, in the limits of these pages, attempting to defend them.

What distinguishes man from the animal world, even the highest of the primates, is that man is both nature and person. Over and above possessing a nature common to his species, as with all other forms of living beings, he possesses an individual personality, the unique and sole 'I', which makes him different from every other person that ever has been or ever can be. His human nature we might compare to the wood on which a sculptor works in order to produce his chosen masterpiece, and his person to the sculptor. His life's task, seen from the point of view of his eternal destiny, is to mould his own particular share of human nature, with all its faults and weaknesses as well as its grandeur and beauty, into the individual masterpiece that God has willed. More specifically, he has to build himself into a fully integrated being, his faculties developed to their fullest potential, his emotions and passions subjugated to the rule of reason, and reason in its turn subjugated to the infinite wisdom and love of the Creator's dominion over all his creatures. Only in this way, when the divine life of Grace infused into him by God has been able to penetrate, unify and transform his whole being, can he be ready for the life of glory, and I would add responsibility, in the new Heaven and the new Earth that will constitute God's household.

Fallen man

Under the best of circumstances this would have been a most difficult and challenging task, but the conditions under which we are called to work out our individual destinies, and to play our share in working out that of the human family as a whole, are very far from ideal. At the earliest dawn of our human family's birth, mankind took a decision not to accept God's dominion. Whatever the truth about the person of Adam, God asked of him something that seemed to him either incomprehensible or else in flat contradiction to the destiny he and all fellow men had been promised. He decided therefore to reject it and instead to take the reins in his own hands. In a word he lacked faith and trust in God who had established such an intimate and lifegiving relationship with him, and lacking faith he fell back upon the light of human reason as his only guide. Having done this he not only excluded any possibility of attaining the eternal destiny to which he had been called, he allowed a principle of evil to enter the world bringing in its train deception, violence and disorder of every imaginable kind, physical as well as spiritual.

Since that most fateful of all days everyone of us has become infected by the same virus, and everyone of us has added our own personal contribution to the totality of discord and lawlessness with which human history has been marred. Within our own very selves we see the evidence of that same conflict, our lower nature struggling to gain control of our higher self, we ourselves unable to do the good that we would and all too often doing what we would not. Even when we do believe we all too easily build our own picture–caricature might be a more accurate word–of who God is. He becomes the God of our own fashioning, not the God of reality. By the same token faith has become weak; we are not even all quite sure what we really mean when we talk about faith. Yet without faith as a foundation on which to build we can never make of our human nature the masterpiece, the unique perfected 'I' that God intended for us. Faith is not just an attitude of mind, an intellectual assent to a truth, to a reality, which though beyond the reach of reason we accept on God's authority. It is an act that operates within the innermost core of our being, a commitment of the whole man, body and soul, to an acceptance of all that the revealed reality involves. In practical terms, faith is our personal response, our 'Yes', to God's covenant with man and thus the indispensable first step in reversing the fatal process initiated by Adam. But if our faith has been lacking during our lifetime, there still remains the hour of our death. Only when we have lived through that hour will the story be finally brought to an end.

Although death is the end, the cutting off of our earthly life, it is in fact already intrinsically present throughout our life, as a fundamental element of all our freely performed actions. That is to say every act that we perform in the moral order, whereby we are free to decide between what is morally right or morally wrong, imparts a direction to our life. We are always declaring what kind of death we wish to die, a death unto God, or a death unto our own autonomous self, in Christian terms either a participation in the redemptive death of Christ or a final denial of our God-given destiny. Death is the final and crucial consummation of that lifelong process of self-determination and struggle for perfection. It is the bringing to maturity of all that a man has made of himself during his lifetime, the taking possession without possibility of self-deception or ambiguity, of his own personality as it has been developed through the conduct of his life, and most particularly in the domain of his freely expressed moral acts. As such it is an interior act of the profoundest meaning and consequence.

The final choice

In our dying, no matter what our life has been–saint or sinner–and no matter what our personal belief or faith–Christian, Moslem, Buddhist, Hindu, atheist to the very core of our being, or anything else under the sun–we are given a final opportunity to choose or reject our eternal destiny. Either we look reality in the face and decide that we wish to become a part of it, or else, whether through defiance, or hatred, or insuperable pride, I really cannot conceive what, we turn our back on it to our eternal ruin. It is either a trusting surrender to the incomprehensible God, who is now slowly revealing himself to us as he really is, or it is a refusal to acknowledge any God other than the God of one's self.

For this reason our dying may be in the fullest and truest sense of the term a mortal sin, a calculated and deliberate refusal to accept the invitation that God still offers, and a final rejection of our eternal destiny. Alternatively it is a humble submission to the living God whom during our lives we have only imperfectly known, and less perfectly still obeyed, but to whom we now turn as our only hope and our only source of fulfilment. There is a tunnel that we will all in our turn have to enter, unless by some great calamity we refuse to do so, choosing instead that abyss which the man who cuts himself off from God becomes. For some the tunnel may be short, for some long and seemingly endless, for the majority, I believe, very dark. But it remains only a tunnel. As gold emerges pure and refined out of fire, so will we emerge out of that mysterious test of faith perfected and transfigured, at peace with the creation and with God, and a co-builder with him of the new Heaven and the new Earth.

Whether we die in an instant without the fraction of a second's warning, or slowly after long and careful preparation, the same holds good, for God is not cheated. He who created time can stretch what to us appears no time at all into all that is needed for a man to consummate his life.

IN THE PRESENCE OF DEATH

In the four years that were to follow Arthur's death, it befell me to sit beside a considerable number of people during the closing hours, or days, of their lives. Writing as I do nearly thirty years later, I cannot claim to have retained an anywhere perfect memory of even the majority of these vigils, though some stand out very vividly and poignantly in my mind. Those who came to that old and rather dilapidated house, Le Court, were of many ages, suffering from a wide variety of illnesses or disability, and professed all kinds of different religious beliefs, some having none at all. Occasionally the end would come very suddenly, catching the sufferer as well as myself almost unawares, but by far the majority lingered on for a long time. Quite a number held on to life with such tenacity–three if not four days after the doctor had said that the end must come at any moment–that this will to live pursued to the utmost limit of human endurance is one of my most lasting impressions. Yet in some cases I felt that it was not merely the will to live but that beneath the external struggle there was taking place another of a different order altogether.

Many, I am afraid to say, died in great pain despite all

that the doctors were able to do. It was these undoubtedly who affected me the most of all, for the dignity which shone through all that was taking place and for the remarkable sense of humour that somehow they managed to retain. Indeed I have come to think that the ability to laugh or to make some kind of a joke and thus break the tension for a brief moment is one of our greatest means of support in moments of severe trial. The occasional one or two were openly aggressive, and at first I was a little hurt, wondering what I had done to provoke them, but it was not me at whom they were getting: what they were really saying was, 'How can God do this to me?', and I came to see that they needed someone against whom they could release their feelings. Some undoubtedly found it very difficult to look death in the face and to accept what they must have known was an inevitable outcome. Yet never, from unbeliever, or believer, came even the slightest passing hint of a wish that their struggle could be shortened. I acknowledge freely that one may reply, 'All very well for you to speak,' but I can only reply that, within my own experience, this is the absolute truth.

Time to sit and share

The friendship which had been forged between Arthur Dykes and myself during the three months or so that we spent together helped me very much and prepared me for the others that were to follow. Nonetheless I continued to feel very inadequate. A priest or a clergyman, I felt, would have done so much better. The little word of spiritual comfort at the moment that it was needed would have come so readily to their lips, but this was not so in my case. I was afraid that no matter how carefully I trod or how sure I was of what I was saying I would sound false and artificial. Instead I fell back on the only thing that I knew I was able to offer, companionship and just the fact of being on hand whenever I was needed. The house had no bells, nor even electricity, and because for many the night seemed to be the loneliest, I took to putting a mattress outside the person's door and giving him a little bell with an assurance that I would not mind how often he rang it. As with Arthur, I found that merely being available and giving the impression that nothing else in the house really mattered at that particular moment except himself and his own individual need—even if at times this was a difficult impression to give—created a very real and personal bond. I also found, as so many others have known even better than I, that physical contact, holding the other person's hand or supporting his head, provided it is a sincere and genuine act and accepted as such, can be a source of great comfort and at times more meaningful than the spoken word. But above everything else I regard time as the best gift one can offer. Time to just sit and share.

In our present Western society time seems to be a precious and rare commodity. We are all too ready to respond to another person's need by doing something for him, perhaps driving a longish distance to perform an errand, or to sort out a problem, or whatever it might be. But just to sit with him for two or three hours for no obvious purpose, other than the fact that this is what he wants, we look upon altogether differently. The same can be said with equal truth about good works and prayer. How easy to fill the day doing something, the object and the results of which we can plainly see. How different to put even a part of the day to one side for prayer or contemplation, without which we may well for all we know be just rushing zig-zag without any clear understanding of the real track we should be following. The person who wants us to sit with him, and who will almost certainly be too sensitive to press his claim, may well be feeling at that particular moment that there is no point at all to his life. What he seeks is reassurance, and if we are willing to give him an hour or two, then our very presence alone gives him the reassurance for which he is looking, is proof that his life means something.

The very fact that medical caution errs on the side of withholding news of a fatal condition from the patient, compounded by our reluctance to talk about death in any shape or form, particularly with the man towards whom its finger is already pointed, means that so many, at the very moment when they most need human comfort and support, find themselves isolated and intensely lonely. Their friends will spend half an evening passing on the news to others and saying what a dreadful thing it is, but they are loath to spend that same time with the person himself. If they do, then they will go to great lengths to avoid the dreaded subject, turning the conversation into safer and more pleasant topics if ever they feel they are getting too close. Curious that men who in other situations are such good judges of what impact a particular statement is likely to have on the other person, are unable to appreciate that in this instance the other man can see through it all only too clearly. He longs to say, 'John, old man, the fact is I haven't really go very long to live. I know there is nothing that anybody can do about it. I don't want to be a burden and I know it is not the kind of thing one ought to talk about, but I would so love to have just somebody with whom I could share it.' But either through consideration for others or simply because he is not sure what the reaction would be, he never says it. Like Oates who stole out of the Antarctic tent so as not to be a nuisance to others, he is left to die alone and in the cold, not through lack of competent hands to nurse and care for him, but through absence of just one person who will share his dying with him.

Again I must be careful not to generalise. Every man's death is a death all of its own, different from anybody else's. One man is rushed to hospital, perhaps to an Intensive Care Unit, where a number of strangers begin to battle for his life so intent upon what they are doing that they may not even stop to ask if there is something he wants, or if indeed he wants the treatment at all. Another goes to one of the specialised Homes where the emphasis is on helping him die his own death in his own way but as free as possible from pain and suffering. Another again will die in his own home amidst familiar surroundings and with his family there to share his dying with him. Not only is every death different from the others, but a man's attitude of mind will change often quite radically during the course of what we term his dying. Anger, envy, deep inward depression, refusal to face the facts, disbelief, sadness are all emotions that may be felt and which therefore the person needs to work through in preparation for final acceptance. On our side it is of great importance not to belittle or pass over these emotions, but rather to try and put ourselves in the other person's position and help him to express them openly and fully. If it is unlikely that all of them will be felt by one individual, I think it is equally unlikely that none of them will be experienced. Clearly a man who has already reached old age, who has completed his duties, whose children have been successfully launched into the world and who can see a purpose and meaning to his life may well be able to face the prospect of death peacefully and perhaps even with a sense of thankfulness. I do not believe, however, that any man can consistently look at death with equanimity. The Christian sees death both as a punishment for sin and as being in opposition to his supernatural destiny, in short the last enemy to be overcome. It is impossible that no matter how great his faith or how holy his life he should not at some time feel an inner, instinctive dread of death, the avenger. Wherever we find him, wherever situated either geographically or in history, man has always looked upon death as something to shrink from, something distasteful. He always surrounds death with a ritual of some kind. Only when we see the stranglehold of death as having been overcome by the redemptive power of Christ's own death can our instinctive fear be replaced by hope. We may confidently assert, whether because of the strength of our faith or the fact that we see death as merely a sinking into oblivion, that we have no fear at all. But I personally find it very difficult to believe that this will prove to be the case when the moment of truth is actually upon us. In any event, what is fear but an occasion to prove our faith and our courage? I do not see why we should be afraid of acknowledging that we too will probably have a moment of dread and of desertion before we render up our soul.

The inner struggle

My lasting impression, as I look back, is that each person, in his own very personal way, underwent an inner struggle at some stage during the process of his dying. Many times have I puzzled over Arthur's strange words: 'I suppose that I shall have to go.' *Where* exactly did he mean, I have asked myself. If ever there was a man who had come to terms with his impending death, who looked towards it in the serene and utter conviction that beyond its gates lay his eternal home in heaven, it was Arthur. Yet when the moment was upon him, after a long period of some inner dialogue within him, he looked puzzled and thoughtful and said as if it were not at all what he had anticipated, 'Yes, I suppose I must go.' They were the words of a man who has been faced with a situation, or a choice, which he was not expecting, which required careful weighing up and to which he could find no other response than agreement. With him at least dying was not just an experience that he underwent passively. It involved both a positive decision and a positive act, and I cannot avoid the conclusion that neither was particularly easy. Yet before his eyes had finally closed in his last sleep a deep peace seemed to have entered the room.

In peace

In every other single case that I can recollect, except perhaps for one, I gained the same impression. Whatever may have been their circumstances or the form that their struggle took during the time of their dying, they all finally died in peace. It was not, I am convinced, a peace of my own wishful thinking, but a peace that one could witness on their face and that in some undefinable way could actually feel. This cannot, I realise, always be true. Clearly it is not when a man dies in mortal agony, as in battle or as a result of some violent physical assault. Equally one must beware of drawing conclusions when a person is heavily sedated or where his behaviour is affected by an unusually toxic disease. But, no matter what the exceptions, I believe that the general rule is true and it seems to me that the experience of those who have spent a large part of their lives in the care of the dying, and who have published their views and findings, bears the same testimony.

Yet even if this be looked upon as an over-generalisation, what is beyond question is that a man's dying is transformed by the companionship and support of someone who is willing to identify with him and stand by his side as long as he should be wanted. The knowledge of our willingness to do this, even if we are not actually in the room at the time, is a source of strength and hope far beyond anything that I suspect we ever imagine. There is an instinct within me, confirmed by what I have heard from others, that even after a man has long lost consiousness he is still in some mysterious way aware of our presence, wanting us to remain and very possibly still able to hear what we say. Never, under any conceivable circumstances, should we say or ask anything in his presence that we would consider an affront to his dignity were he conscious. His self-respect, his right to share in any decision that affects him insofar as this is possible, and his human dignity, we should uphold to the very last moment.

There remains finally the other side of the story. To accompany a man on his final life's steps as a companion and a friend, recognising that it is his special hour in which we are privileged to share, is to receive as much as it is to give. It is to become more of a man oneself, more fulfilled and mature, and almost certainly a little more sensitive to what is taking place in another person's heart. It is to learn how truly our living and our dying are both part and parcel of the same process and how much easier it would all become if we could learn to talk about it during our lifetime as naturally and realistically as we do with life's other main turning points.

RESURRECTION

Bede Jarrett OP

THE RESURRECTION

Rev. Bede Jarrett, O.P.

The mystery of Christ our Lord's resurrection must always give a note of hopefulness to the Christian's outlook upon all life. No follower of that risen Master can ever consistently with his faith look with eyes of mere foreboding on the future of the race or of himself. Always there will be that final scene of the Gospel story heartening him, and beckoning to him to hold fast to belief in the final triumph of good, which is of course the final triumph of God. No life, no cause can ever appear so hopelessly defeated as that which seemingly ended on Calvary amid the mockery, the laughter, the darkness, and death-cry; no one can ever be quite so badly situated as that Master was, that Patriot, the Lover, when betrayed, denied, abandoned (save for His mother, a young and dreamy friend, and a rescued woman) He bowed His head on the Cross.

Yet defeat was turned to triumph; death to life; and a final dawn dispelled all the darkness. After that, no one has ever any excuse for any fearful view of an ultimate defeat of his hopes or ideals, so long as he can hold these to be the ideals of God. After that, we can be sure that freedom and justice and truth must, despite every delay or obstruction, win in the end; and when that end comes, then the bitter sufferings of this life are easily seen to be far outbalanced by the exceeding weight of glory, revealed hereafter.

This is of course the firm hope that has all along upheld the Christian people in their darkest hours; and even in the earliest ages it was to the Resurrection that they confidently appealed as the final judgement passed by God upon life. Consequently it is easily realized how enormously important it must be to be sure of the truth of the Resurrection. We base our final hopes, our faith, on this as the true judgement on life; then how very careful we have to be to make sure that our hopes and faith are justified. The Christian builds up his edifice upon these foundations and is cheered in his moments of obstruction and delay, in the wearisome business of building, by the knowledge that finally his work will stand because it is built upon a rock. He is therefore correspondingly interested in the question whether after all it is a rock, whether the basic fact is in utter reality a fact at all.

Now the argument to defend the truth of the Resurrection is perhaps more carefully arranged by St. Thomas Aquinas than by any other theologian; and to save the prolonged and lengthy process of showing in detail every step of the proof it will be simpler just to set out in the form of a scheme all the various converging evidences which he has so thoughtfully adjusted. But of course the reader should take into his hands the Gospels and refer to each text cited and so see for himself the massive proof gradually rising and showing its firm outlines clear against the sky. The article in which St. Thomas treats of the Resurrection is taken from his *Summa Theologica* (Part III, Q. 55, Art. 6), and will be found in the English translation: Part III, Second Number, pp. 412-417. It is a very perfect example of the power possessed by St. Thomas of marshalling evidence and proofs till they produce an overwhelming conviction.

St. Thomas's own commentary on this scheme may be quoted from his answer to the first objection which he brings against it (p. 414): "Each separate argument would not suffice of itself for showing perfectly Christ's Resurrection, yet all taken collectively establish it completely."

To this should be added the argument given by St. Paul as to the actual witnesses who saw the risen Christ:

"For I delivered unto you first of all which I also received: how that Christ died for our sins according to the Scriptures; and that He was buried, and that He rose again the third day according to the Scriptures: and that He was seen by Cephas, and after that by the eleven. Then was He seen by more than five hundred brethren at once; of whom many remain until this present, and some are fallen asleep. After that He was seen by James, then by all the Apostles; and last of all He was seen also by me" (I Cor. xv. 3-8).

Here then we have St. Paul setting out very carefully a list of people by name who could then mostly have been consulted for their evidence of the facts, could have been cross-examined and their replies sifted. Of course we are not so situated as were these Corinthians and we cannot go directly to see and talk with people who with their own eyes saw their Redeemer in His risen flesh. Yet Our Lord has forestalled any complaints that we might be thereby led to make by saying to St. Thomas the Apostle: "Because thou hast seen Me, Thomas, thou hast believed: blessed are they that have not seen, and have believed" (John xx. 29). Moreover, the exceedingly careful way in which St. Paul has gathered and arranged his evidence, helps enormously to bear out the details, unconsciously hinted at as well as deliberately described in the various accounts given us in the Gospels.

Further, it should be added here that the apparent contradictions in the order of Our Lord's risen appearances, as given in these Gospels (such as opponents of Christianity love to exhibit) is due entirely to the fragmentary character of their narrative. However the following harmony of these witnesses has been taken from Father Hugh Pope's *Aids to the Study of the Bible,* vol. ii, pp. 348-350:

I.–THE VISITS OF THE HOLY WOMEN:

(a) Our Lord appears to St. Mary Magdalen first (Mark xvi. 9-11).

(b) Several of them visit the Sepulchre (Matt. xxviii. i: Mark xvi. 1-2: Luke xxiv. 1).

THE EVIDENCES FOR THE RESURRECTION

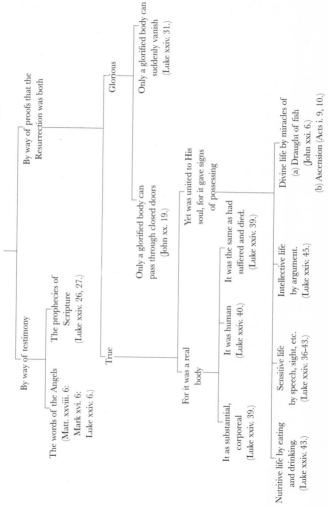

By way of testimony

The words of the Angels
(Matt. xxviii. 6;
Mark xvi. 6;
Luke xxiv. 6.)

The prophecies of
Scripture
(Luke xxiv. 26, 27.)

By way of proofs that the
Resurrection was both

True

Glorious

Only a glorified body can
pass through closed doors
(John xx. 19.)

Only a glorified body can
suddenly vanish
(Luke xxiv. 31.)

Yet was united to His
soul, for it gave signs
of possessing

For it was a real
body

It was the same as had
suffered and died.
(Luke xxiv. 39.)

It as substantial,
corporeal
(Luke xxiv. 39.)

It was human
(Luke xxiv. 40.)

Nutritive life by eating
and drinking.
(Luke xxiv. 43.)

Sensitive life
by speech, sight, etc.
(Luke xxiv. 36-43.)

Intellective life
by argument.
(Luke xxiv. 45.)

Divine life by miracles of
(a) Draught of fish
John xxi. 6.)
(b) Ascension (Acts i. 9, 10.)

(c) They find the stone rolled away (Matt. xxviii. 2: Mark xvi. 3-4: Luke xxiv. 2: John xx. 2).

(d) The guards are terrified (Matt. xxviii. 4).

(e) The Vision of the Angels and their message that He is risen and shall be seen in Galilee (Matt. xxviii. 5-7; Mark xvi. 5-7: Luke xxiv. 4-7).

(f) Our Lord appears and gives the same message (Matt. xxviii. 9-10).

(g) The women's message to the disciples (Mark xvi. 8: Luke xxiv. 9-10: John xx. 2, 18).

(h) The incredulity of the disciples (Matt. xxviii. 17: Mark xvi. 11, 13, 14: Luke xi. 11-14: John xx. 3-10).

II.—OTHER APPARITIONS:

(a) Peter and John run to the Sepulchre (Luke xxiv. 12: John xx. 3-10).

(b) Guards are bribed to silence (Matt. xxviii. 11-15).

(c) He appears to Cleophas and another on way to Emmaus (Mark xvi. 12: Luke xxiv. 13-35).

(d) He appears to Cephas [Peter] (Luke xxiv. 34: I Cor. xv. 5).

(e) He appears to disciples in Supper-room (Luke xxiv. 36-43: John xx. 19-23).

(f) He appears again to convince St. Thomas (John xx. 24-29).

(g) He appears to seven disciples by lake-side (John xxi. 1-23).

In this way we can piece together the separated items in the various accounts of what took place and form for ourselves a detailed and graphic picture of the Resurrection, which has also the merit of being authenticated by the primitive documentary lives of Our Lord.

Perhaps it is well also to realize that this belief in the resurrection or resuscitation of Our Lord after death is taught by all the four Gospels and by them in passages which have never been challenged as unauthentic by the scriptural critics. Thus although the last verses of St. Mark's Gospel and the last verses too of St. John's Gospel have sometimes been held to be additions by early disciples and not part of the primitive text, even so (1) these additions are evidences of the belief of the early disciples and (2) in other passages of the same Gospel (Mark xvi, 1-8: John xx. 1-29) the doctrine is taught. St. Paul again is perpetually insisting upon it as a matter of the common belief of all Christians. The Acts of the Apostles (xiii. 27-34: xvii. 31: xxvi. 23) tell us the main lines of his message and their witness is borne out by his epistles. Compare for instance in Acts xvii. 2 etc. the account given of his preaching to the Thessalonians with his own first letter to the Thessalonians (1 Thess. i. 9-10) and it will be clear that he puts this doctrine in the forefront of the Christian's creed. Moreover he adds that it is something which he has himself 'received' or been taught, and quotes, as we have seen, the two

Apostles Peter and James (cf. also Gal. i. 18-20) as original witnesses from whom he obtained an account of the various apparitions of the risen Christ. Finally he adduces the apparition of Christ made to himself on the road to Damascus partly as a confirmation of the belief of the Apostles and partly as a proof of his own apostolate (cf. Acts xxvi. 10-20: I Cor. xv. 8) for an apostle in the Gospel sense of the word must be one who was "a witness of His resurrection." (Acts i. 22: Acts ii. 22-32: iii. 15: v. 30-32: x. 39-41. Compare also I Peter i. 3 and i. 21).

From the official statements that we have of the actual preaching of the Apostles and of the creed which they expounded to their converts we can definitely and absolutely assert

(1) that it is historically certain that from the beginnings of Christianity the disciples believed and proclaimed that Christ had risen from the dead;

(2) that it is historically certain that this belief implied His *bodily* resurrection (see p. 4). Even those who deny this doctrine cannot deny that it is primitive and clearly accepted by the first disciples;

(3) that it is historically certain that the primitive belief of these disciples also included the further point of the resurrection having taken place "on the third day."

These statements are irrefutable. Moreover we can see from the biblical accounts of the resurrection that two facts are to be added to these, namely the assertions that Christ was buried and that after He rose again the tomb was empty. It does not seem that these have been challenged by the critics as later additions to the original simple creed. They figure in the Gospel accounts and in St. Paul's Epistles: and between them we are compelled to accept the conclusion that the Apostles never contemplated a resurrection, which was purely spiritual or symbolic but one which was literal and historic.

If then the New Testament is to be taken in any sense whatever as a statement of early Christianity, it is not reasonable or honourable to speak of the bodily apparitions of Christ as the invention of later and more uncritical times. If it is an invention it is an invention that dates from the beginning. If it is a misunderstanding of what happened, then it is a misunderstanding that rose from contemplating an empty tomb. Various theories have been suggested to explain away this doctrine of the resurrection, principally three;

(a) It has been supposed that the Apostles knew of the doctrine from pagan mythologies of Babylonia or Phœnicia or Egypt or the Roman Attis or the Greek Dionysios. But this is a mere supposition. Scholars are forced to admit that in the Judaism of the time of Christ there is no trace of any influence of these cults.

(b) It has been urged that the teaching of the Old Testament was sufficient to give the Apostles the idea of a resurrection. But though it is true that the prophecies of the Old Testament do proclaim the resurrection of the Messias it is no less true that the Apostles were completely blind to this till after the resurrection had taken place. During Our Lord's lifetime they repudiated it (Matt. xvi. 21: Mark viii. 31: John xx. 9: Luke xxiv. 25, 26, 27); only after His resurrection did they remember what had been taught them. The women came out therefore to anoint a dead body. When Magdalen found the tomb empty, she could only suppose He had been *taken* away. So little were any of them expecting this issue that when these women came back to the Apostles with the story of the empty tomb and the angel, "these words seemed to them idle tales; and they did not believe them" (Luke xxiv. 11). Moreover the state of mind of the two who were going to Emmaus and the very reason why they were leaving Jerusalem for Emmaus again implies the very opposite of any such expectation. Psychologically they needed very definite proofs of the resurrection before any of them would believe.

(c) The prevailing scepticism of the critics of to-day is shown by their reverting to the Jewish story of the second century that the body was removed from the tomb by Joseph of Arimathea to prevent his lettuces and cabbages from being trodden down by the disciples!! Other once popular "explanations" have now been abandoned by the critics as foolish and unreasonable; they have come back to this which is supported by no single proof of any kind whatsoever. Moreover Joseph had already braved Pilate's anger by asking to have the body buried and having obtained it could have placed it where it would have been more easily abstracted than his own family grave. If he intended to remove the body later or to bide it, he made his task difficult, was watched by the soldiers, and apparently disposed of the body so completely that no breath or whisper of tradition has ever hinted of the real resting place of one whose name grew to be glorious and over every detail of whose life and words countless millions have studied, pondered, and prayed.

Every conceivable explanation has been tried in order to escape the truth of the belief of the Apostles, and none of them has proved to be really acceptable for long to scholars. None of the hypotheses proposed in the last hundred years are still generally accepted by critics. None are plausible. None have any shred of evidence to support them. Frankly they are put forward to explain away something which seems impossible to the critics; but in effect they do not really explain it in accordance with the acknowledged story and known facts.

Even the theory of hallucinations can no longer be

accepted by the modern psychologist, for hallucinations have been proved now only to strengthen impressions already accepted in the normal state. Hallucinations do not come against the judgement but in accordance with it. Hence only in so far as the Apostles hoped for and expected a resurrection would they have had hallucinations which convinced them of it: whereas all of them, including St. Paul on the road to Damascus, were convinced of the truth of the resurrection against their normal state of judgment. Psychologically it is not possible to account for the story by using the word "hallucinations" as used once to be the fashion; psychology has here apparently confounded the critics and upheld the truth. Indeed it is only because the critics are determined to deny the resurrection that they are driven to these shifts and unscholarly devices to explain the origin of the belief. They dislike the miraculous and for that reason say it cannot be. They rest their case not on scientific observation but on a metaphysical prejudice. It is not because miracles have not been observed that these people deny them but only because they lay down a definite law that miracles cannot happen. Instead of accepting the prolonged experience of the miraculous and making room for it which science must do sooner or later, they merely obstinately deny that it can be. They are here no longer scientists but dogmatists. They are definitely prejudiced; that is, they prejudge the matter before approaching it. These obviously can only be convinced by some change of philosophy: accumulation of evidence will not compel them. They are impervious to facts. Thus the modernist Theological school is definitely pledged to a philosophy which contradicts the whole spirit of the New Testament. It is not Christian. It cannot prevail.

The fact then that He rose triumphant over death is established. We can now proceed to consider what we are to conclude from this. These conclusions will be found to be twofold, first as regards the witness it brings to our Blessed Lord's divinity, and secondly as regards the actual personal application it has to us.

First then, how does it effect Our Lord's own position? It affects it immediately and vitally, for while the death of Christ might be taken to imply that He was in no way different from other men, His triumph over death could have no other meaning than the significant challenge of His claim to unique divinity. To die in defence of one's belief is evidence indeed of sincerity, but it cannot demonstrate the authenticity of that conviction, since men have died for contradictory beliefs. Martyrdom proves that the martyr believes what he says; it does not prove however that what he says is true. That Christ was sincere cannot be denied; the conclusion that He was therefore divine happens actually in this case to be logical, for one who sincerely believes Himself to be God, and, paradoxically, dies to prove it, must either be hopelessly insane or really divine. But the final touch is given to the argument and all the proof rendered irresistible when to it is added the reappearance of the dead Christ, still clothed and habited in a human body, but now wonderfully alive, eating, and speaking, and showing this way and that the very wounds that were His undoing. For the argument has now a new witness to support His claim: Our Lord claimed to be God, died to attest the sincerity of His claim, was raised up to life again by divine power (either His own or Another's) in testimony of the truth of His doctrine. The Author of Life and Death has therefore added His own witness to the witness of Christ. God has sealed by His power the declaration of His Son. If Christ were not God, then God Himself must have been a party to the deceit practised on the human race. We can prove the historic truth of the Resurrection. Either, then, this took place by Our Lord's own power or by God's power. In the first case, He is divine; and in the second, God must have wished to ratify Our Lord's claim to be divine.

For us Catholics, therefore, the historic side of the mystery must never be allowed to become obscure. But the historic side is of value to us also, not only for what it says but for what it implies. There is undoubtedly a mystical meaning that lies hid within the facts of faith. The new birth, the rising sap of the spring, the feeling of hope with which at this season of the year creation tingles, are all contained in the very notion of Easter and its festive interpretation. In the spirit generated by feelings so intensely alive and eager, death is seen in its true proportion, not as the ending of man's existence, but as a mere incident in its process, painful indeed, lonely, testing his labours and his intentions, yet to be accepted as a necessary stage and in that process not the most important. Three days in the tomb, or really only part of three days, are a very short period to be set off against eternity. So comes there to the Christian soul a deep feeling of the inner mysteries of Easter. He is bidden to look forward to the new Life, not back to the wasted and fallen years. The past is past: let the dead bury their dead; for there is a future as well that is considerably more important to him, a future for which he was created and in which alone shall he ever be fully satisfied. Here until death comes there must always be a misfit; always the soul must feel out-at-elbows, for it is too large to be crampt with comfort into mere mortal existence. Swaddling bands straiten us at our beginnings on earth, the winding-sheet holds us grimly at the close; and during the years that lapse between the one and the other we are conscious of the "prison-house" about us. It is only after we have passed beyond it that we shall know what true freedom means.

But the Resurrection of Our Lord not only promises for us a future; it gives us a true effective philosophy to guide us even at present on earth. It announces for ever the wholly Christian doctrine of a final hope for the world— final not only in the sense that somewhere at last all the balance of injustice and failure and defeat, suffered so frequently by the good here, will eventually be set right; but that even on earth there will repeatedly recur the resurrection of some crucified ideal. The Church is just such another case where from time to time the hand of God is made visible in His creation and the doomed mystic body becomes transfigured and once more, after death, alive. So the ideals of truth which generations have criticized, mocked, and denounced, are suddenly found to have reappeared with honour among men. So freedom after nightmares of tyranny wakes and stretches and stirs herself. So nations, oppressed and broken, once more are found in their places, made whole and vigorous.

But this mystery of faith has a meaning really even more intimate than that, in its steady, unfailing witness to the vitality of life; for to the individual no less than to groups of people, the Resurrection brings its message of hope. It promises him for himself, through the mercy and power of God, a perpetual miracle of new life through hope and faith and love. Even for those who are dead in sin, we have this deeper and nobler assurance: "O death, where is thy victory? O death, where is thy sting? Death is swallowed up in victory, thanks be to God, who hath given us the victory through Our Lord Jesus Christ" (1 Cor. xv. 54-57).

BACKGROUND

Although Leonard Cheshire's remarkable and heroic war service (he flew over a hundred bombing missions over Germany and occupied Europe and was awarded a string of decorations, including the Victoria Cross) had made death a daily companion, it was not until after the war, when he was called to the bedside of a dying comrade from the RAF, that he first saw it clearly, and recognised the value of accompanying the dying as a form of Christian love. The well-known "Cheshire Homes" for the disabled are a lasting memorial to his work.

Bede Jarrett was Provincial of the Dominican Order in England from 1916 until his death. His booklet on the resurrection offers a forensic defence of the teaching, and its relevance to ourselves. It is perhaps telling that it was first published in 1919, immediately after the Great War, when death and its sequels were a present reality for most of the population.

CTS ONEFIFTIES